How to Draw
Crazy
Machines
and Other Cool Stuff

Green Android

Created and produced by Green Android Ltd

Illustrated by Fiona Gowen

Green Android Ltd
49 Beaumont Court
Upper Clapton Road
London E5 8BG
United Kingdom
www.greenandroid.co.uk

ISBN 978-1-909244-01-6

Printed and bound in Dongguan, China, May 2014

Contents

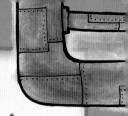

 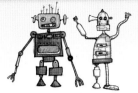
Page 32 has an index of everything to draw in this book.

How to Draw
Walking Robots

One day robots could help us do all sorts of jobs like cooking and cleaning. When you draw robots it's fun to make them look a bit like humans as this gives them personality.

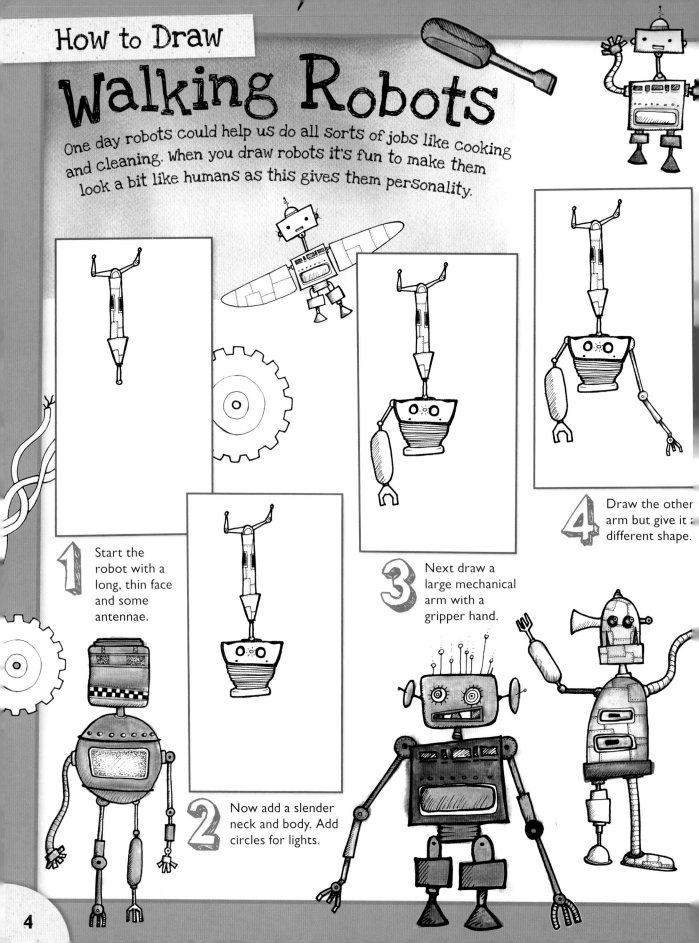

1 Start the robot with a long, thin face and some antennae.

2 Now add a slender neck and body. Add circles for lights.

3 Next draw a large mechanical arm with a gripper hand.

4 Draw the other arm but give it a different shape.

4

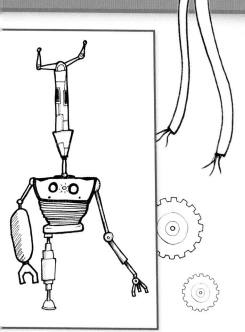

More to Draw

Mix and match these body parts to make more robots. You could draw a whole robot family!

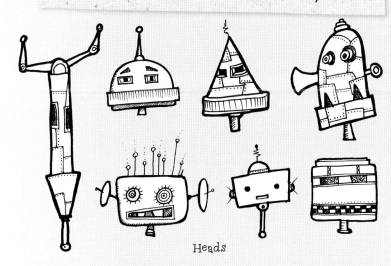

Heads

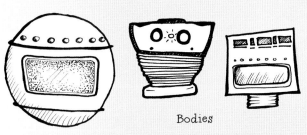

Bodies

5 Now you can add one of the legs. Make it look hydraulic with a suction cup for a foot.

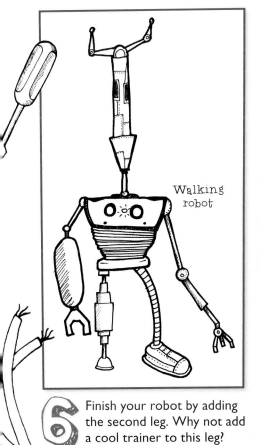

Walking robot

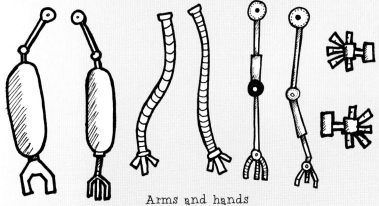

Arms and hands

6 Finish your robot by adding the second leg. Why not add a cool trainer to this leg?

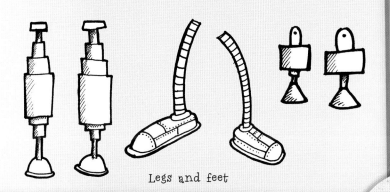

Legs and feet

5

Wheely Robots

Robots with wheels could be used for many different jobs. Try to make your robot look as though it could travel around incredibly fast.

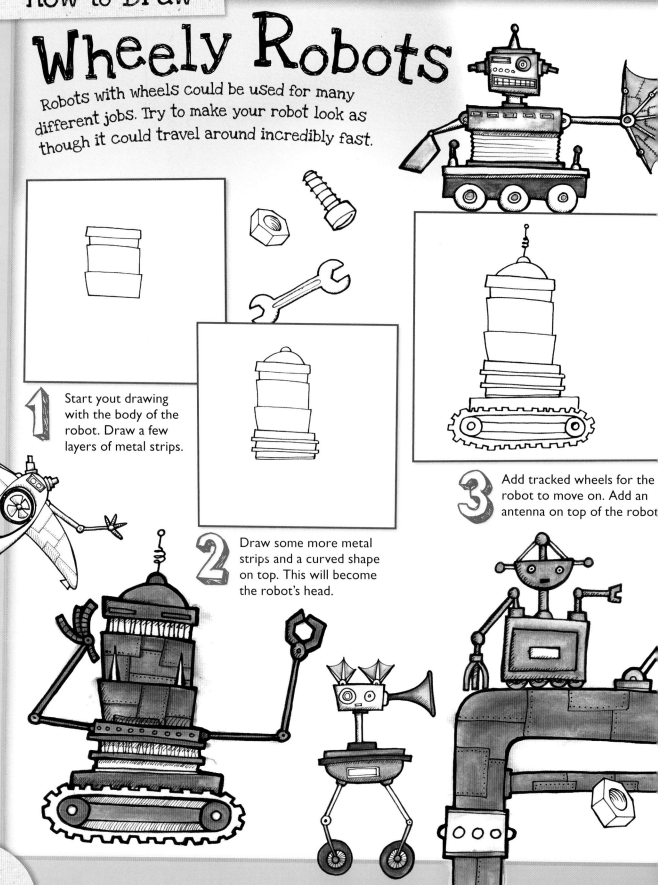

1 Start yout drawing with the body of the robot. Draw a few layers of metal strips.

2 Draw some more metal strips and a curved shape on top. This will become the robot's head.

3 Add tracked wheels for the robot to move on. Add an antenna on top of the robot

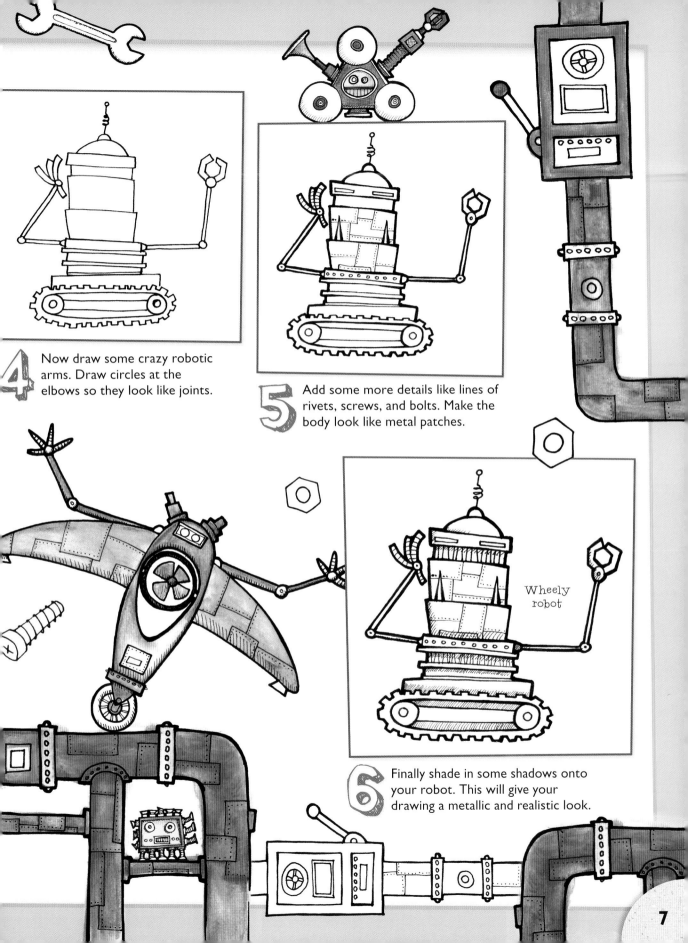

Now draw some crazy robotic arms. Draw circles at the elbows so they look like joints.

Add some more details like lines of rivets, screws, and bolts. Make the body look like metal patches.

Wheely robot

Finally shade in some shadows onto your robot. This will give your drawing a metallic and realistic look.

Groovy Guitars

Every rock band needs a great guitarist. The electric guitar is a fantastic instrument to play and one of the coolest things to draw!

Microphone

3 Draw the head. This is where the strings are attached and tuned.

1 Start your guitar with a thin rectangle for the neck.

Combination amp

2 Now add a crazy shape for the body of your rock guitar.

Practice amp

4 Draw some small rectangles on the main body of the guitar.

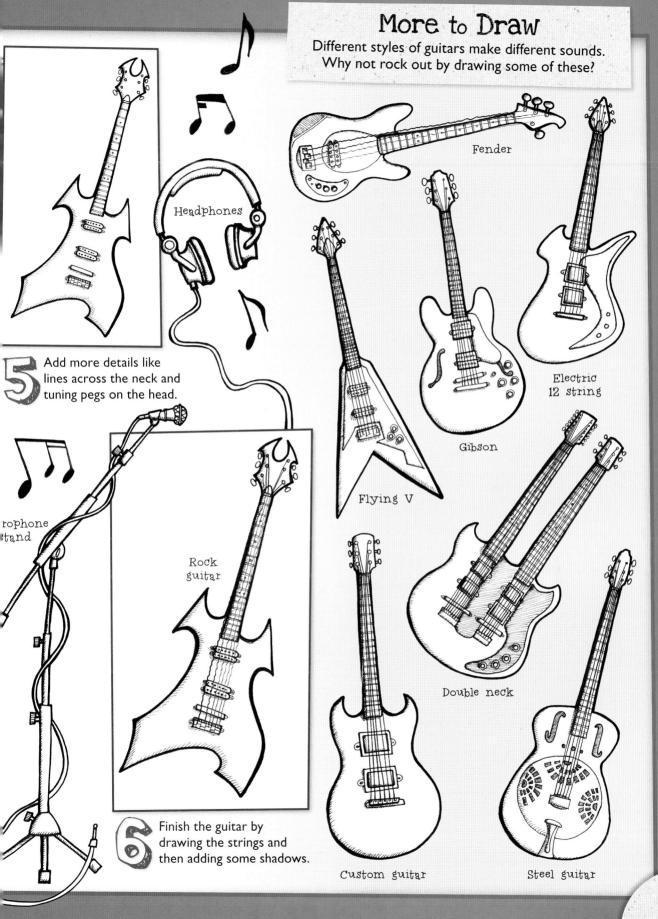

More to Draw

Different styles of guitars make different sounds.
Why not rock out by drawing some of these?

Headphones

Fender

Electric
12 string

5 Add more details like lines across the neck and tuning pegs on the head.

Gibson

Flying V

rophone
tand

Rock guitar

Double neck

6 Finish the guitar by drawing the strings and then adding some shadows.

Custom guitar

Steel guitar

How to Draw

Incredible Cranes

Construction sites are noisy places that are full of amazing vehicles and weird machinery. Start your construction drawing with this crane.

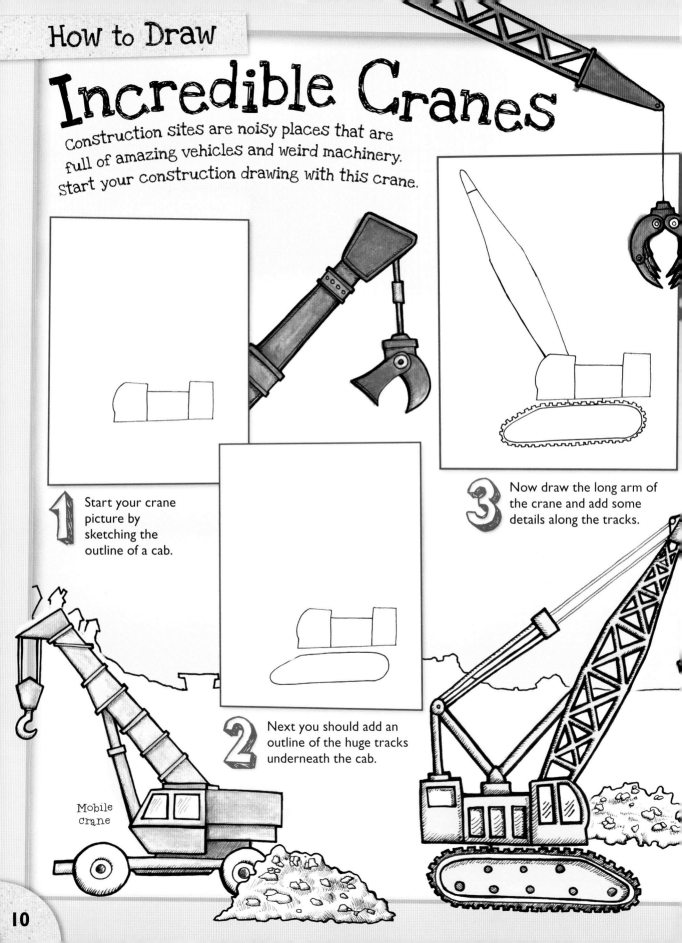

1 Start your crane picture by sketching the outline of a cab.

2 Next you should add an outline of the huge tracks underneath the cab.

3 Now draw the long arm of the crane and add some details along the tracks.

Mobile crane

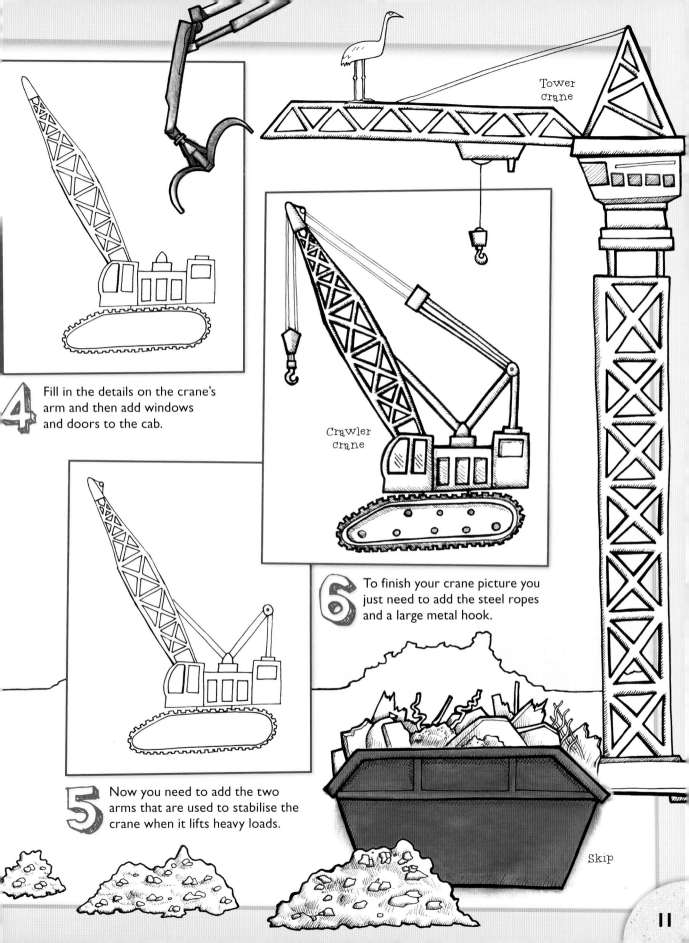

Tower crane

4 Fill in the details on the crane's arm and then add windows and doors to the cab.

Crawler crane

6 To finish your crane picture you just need to add the steel ropes and a large metal hook.

5 Now you need to add the two arms that are used to stabilise the crane when it lifts heavy loads.

Skip

How to Draw

Awesome Gadgets

There are a lot of cool gadgets to play with. By pressing a few buttons we can surf the internet, talk to friends, watch TV, play games and much, much more!

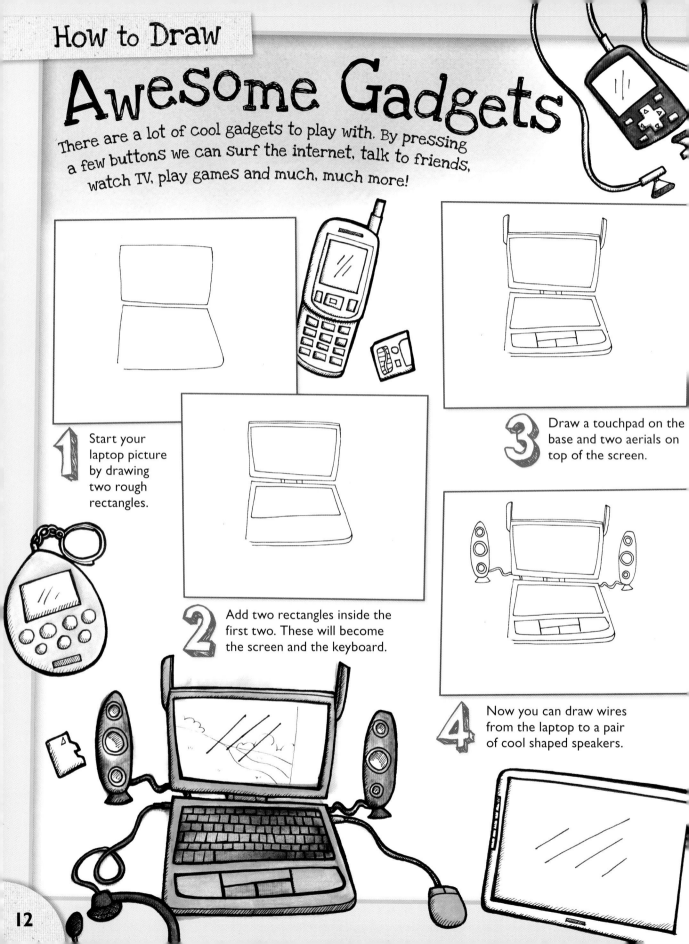

1 Start your laptop picture by drawing two rough rectangles.

2 Add two rectangles inside the first two. These will become the screen and the keyboard.

3 Draw a touchpad on the base and two aerials on top of the screen.

4 Now you can draw wires from the laptop to a pair of cool shaped speakers.

There are some amazing electrical gadgets.
Draw all the cool gadgets you'd like to use.

Keyring game

Tablet computer

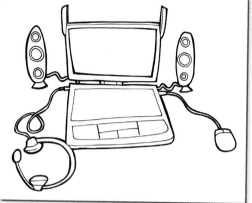

5 Draw a mouse, a set of
headphones and a microphone.
Join these to the laptop with wires.

Flip phone

Touch-screen
phone

Slide phone

Laptop
computer

Walkie-talkies

MP3 player

6 To finish the drawing add
shadows to the laptop and then
sketch a scene onto the screen.

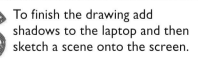

Memory card

USB
memory
stick

Flash card

Hand-held game

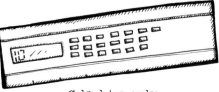

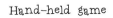

Calculator ruler

Crazy Vacuums

We use lots of different household machines every day. When drawing this fun vacuum picture try to make the hose look like it's out of control!

1 Start your drawing with the base and a set of wheels.

2 Draw the body of the vacuum cleaner. Leave a gap on the left side.

3 Add a lid on top of the cleaner and a socket on the side of the body.

4 Now draw a hose coming from the body of the cleaner.

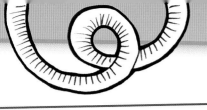

More to Draw
Vacuum cleaners come in all sorts of shapes and sizes.
Try drawing some of these models.

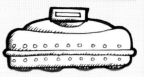

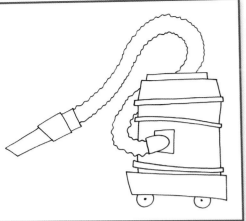

Hand-held
vacuum

Robotic vacuum

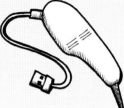

USB vacuum

Hovering
vacuum

5 You can add a nozzle to the
end of the hose. Your drawing
is now nearly finished.

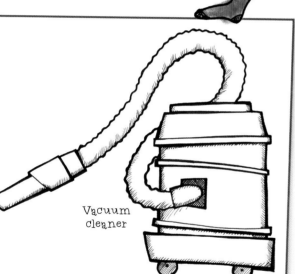

Vacuum
cleaner

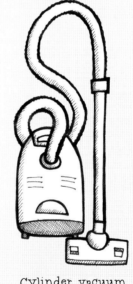

Cylinder vacuum

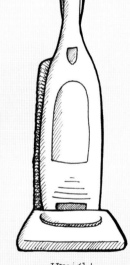

Upright
vacuum

6 To finish the drawing go over the lines
and add some shading. This will help
to make your picture look realistic.

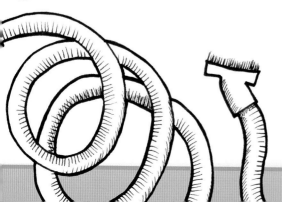

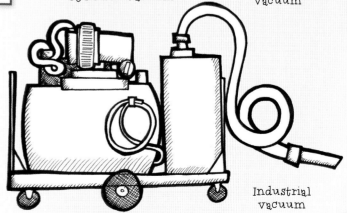

Industrial
vacuum

Fantastic Cameras

There are many types of cameras to choose from.
Older cameras use film, while newer cameras
are digital and are used with a computer.

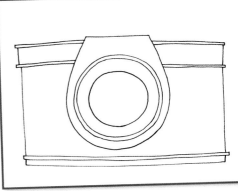

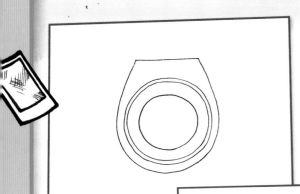

1 Start your drawing with the lens of the camera.

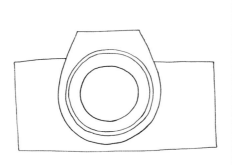

2 Now draw a rectangle behind the lens for the body of the camera.

3 Add some extra layers on top and underneath the body of the camera.

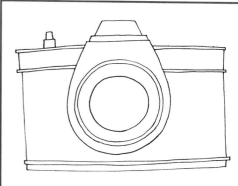

4 You can add a shape to the top of the lens and also add a button.

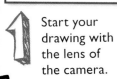

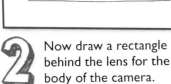

More to Draw
We have been taking photos for over a hundred years.
Try drawing some of these different cameras.

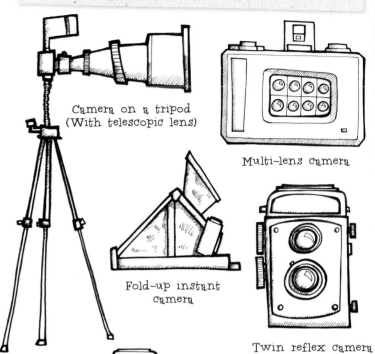

Camera on a tripod
(With telescopic lens)

Multi-lens camera

5 Draw some more details around the button and add a reflected shape onto the lens.

Fold-up instant camera

Twin reflex camera

Panoramic camera

Instant camera

35mm SLR

6 Finish the camera by shading the body darker than the top. Then add shadows for a realistic look.

Jigsaw camera

Vintage camera

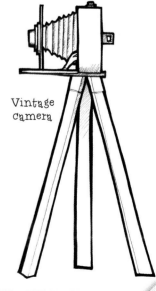

Fisheye camera

Science Stuff

Science experiments are exciting as you are never sure what you might discover. When drawing science laboratories you can let your imagination go wild!

Funnel

Measuring cylinder

Flask

1 Start your drawing with an outline of the arm of the microscope.

2 Add the viewing lens and the flatbed. Join the flatbed to the arm.

3 You can now create a big, sturdy base for your microscope to sit on.

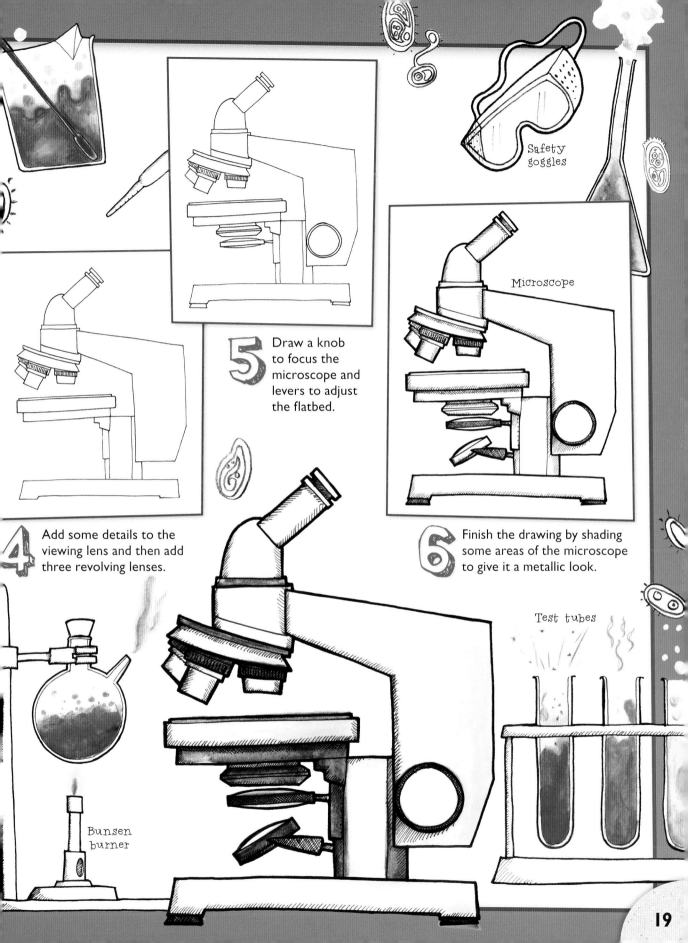

Safety
goggles

5 Draw a knob
to focus the
microscope and
levers to adjust
the flatbed.

Microscope

4 Add some details to the
viewing lens and then add
three revolving lenses.

6 Finish the drawing by shading
some areas of the microscope
to give it a metallic look.

Test tubes

Bunsen
burner

How to Draw
Kitchen Workers

Kitchen blenders can make cooking fun and easy. They can be used to blend, puree, liquidise and chop. Imagine what delicious things you could make with your blender.

1 Start by drawing the container at the top.

2 Add the base of the blender. This section contains the motor.

3 Draw a handle and lid onto the container and some small feet onto the base.

4 Add a switch and dial onto the base. Draw a measurement li down the side of the contain

Kitchens are full of crazy machines that help us cook.
Which other kitchen machines can you think of?

5 Now make the outline of the drawing thicker by going over it again with a pencil.

Kettle

Coffee maker

Hand-held blender

Deep fat fryer

Smoothie maker

Blender

Juicer

Whisk

6 Finish the drawing by adding fruits or vegetables inside the container. Now you're ready to cook!

Slow cooker

Microwave oven

Steamer

Treasure Hunters

People use metal detectors to find all sorts of buried treasure. You could be lucky and find an ancient coin or a priceless gold watch!

1 Start your drawing with the handle of the metal detector.

2 Draw the two parts of the metal detector's shaft coming out of the handle.

3 Add a search coil at the bottom, a control box in the middle and the stabiliser at the top of the shaft.

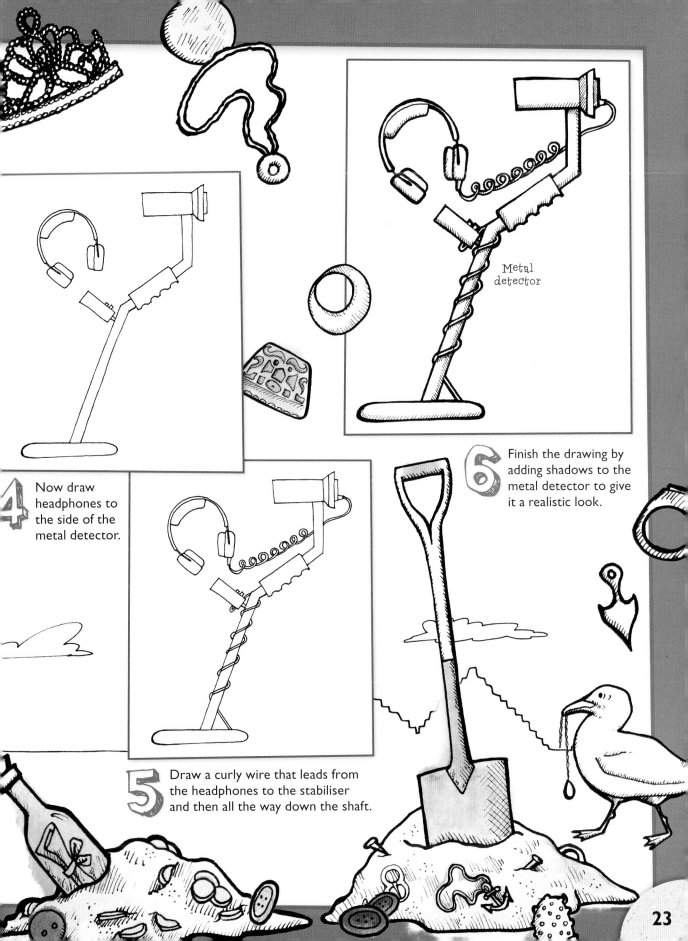

Metal detector

4 Now draw headphones to the side of the metal detector.

5 Draw a curly wire that leads from the headphones to the stabiliser and then all the way down the shaft.

6 Finish the drawing by adding shadows to the metal detector to give it a realistic look.

Amazing Telescopes

Astronomers use large telescopes to look up into the night sky. They learn all about space, the stars and other planets in our solar system.

Compound telescope

1 Start by drawing the telescope's large lens.

2 Add the rest of the body of the telescope. Leave a gap at the bottom of the body.

3 Now draw the dials that are used to adjust the telescope.

Communication satellite

Binoc

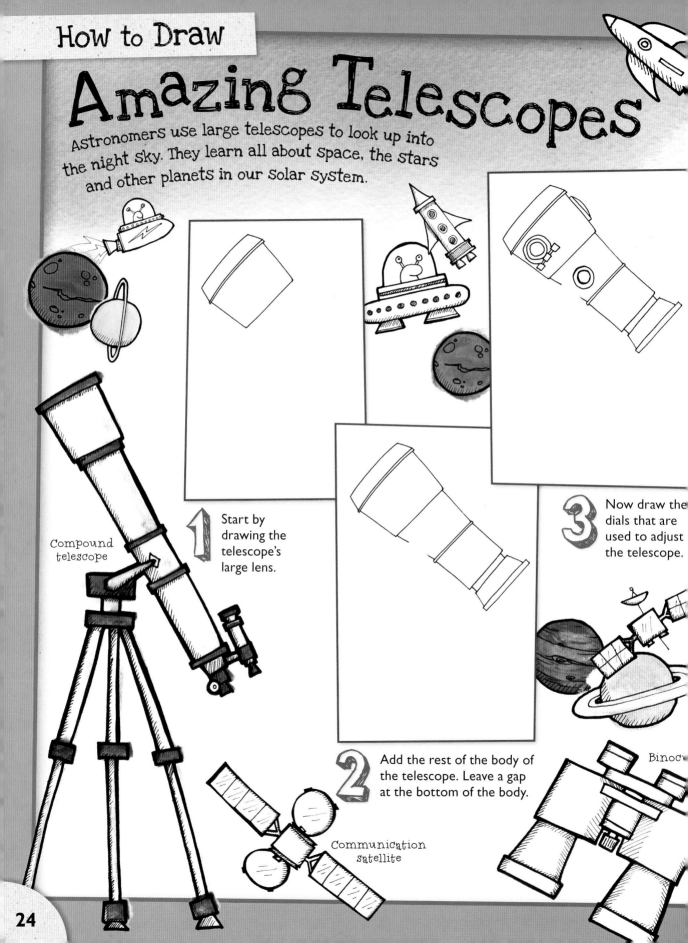

24

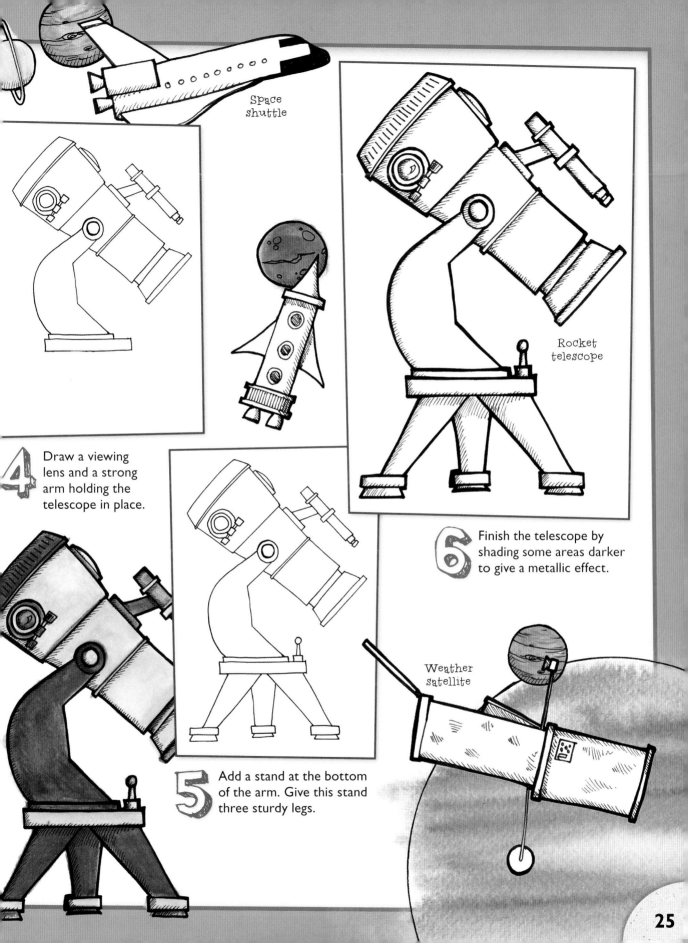

Space shuttle

Rocket telescope

Weather satellite

4 Draw a viewing lens and a strong arm holding the telescope in place.

5 Add a stand at the bottom of the arm. Give this stand three sturdy legs.

6 Finish the telescope by shading some areas darker to give a metallic effect.

How to Draw

Grand Clocks

We use a lot of different machines to tell the time. Older clocks, like this grandfather clock, need to be wound up each day in order to keep the correct time.

1 Start your drawing with a square for the clock's face.

2 Now begin to draw a frame around the clock face.

3 Add a curved top above the clock face and two columns underneath.

4 Draw some ornate patterns onto the top and base.

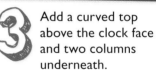

II

VIII

More to Draw

There are lots of different ways to tell the time.
Why not try drawing some of these?

Grandfather clock

5 Add hands to the clock and a swinging pendulum and weights.

XII

6 Finish by adding details to the clock face and shading some areas.

Cuckoo clock

Pocket watch

Wrist watch

Alarm clock

Shop clock

Sun dial

Sand timer

Workshop Tools

To build most things we need to use power tools. Power tools make work much easier and a lot quicker than old fashioned manual tools.

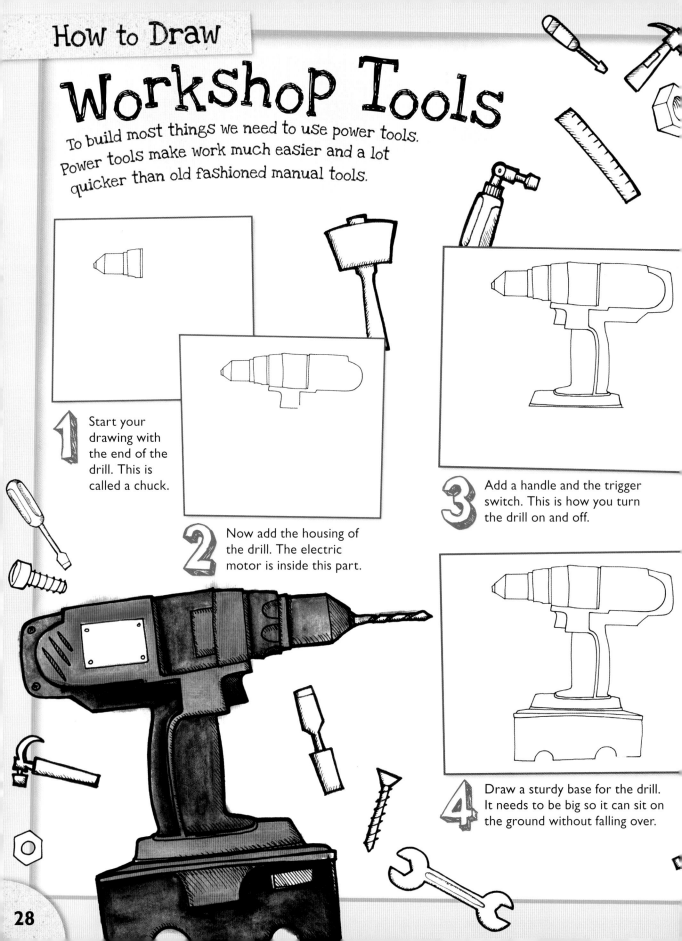

1 Start your drawing with the end of the drill. This is called a chuck.

2 Now add the housing of the drill. The electric motor is inside this part.

3 Add a handle and the trigger switch. This is how you turn the drill on and off.

4 Draw a sturdy base for the drill. It needs to be big so it can sit on the ground without falling over.

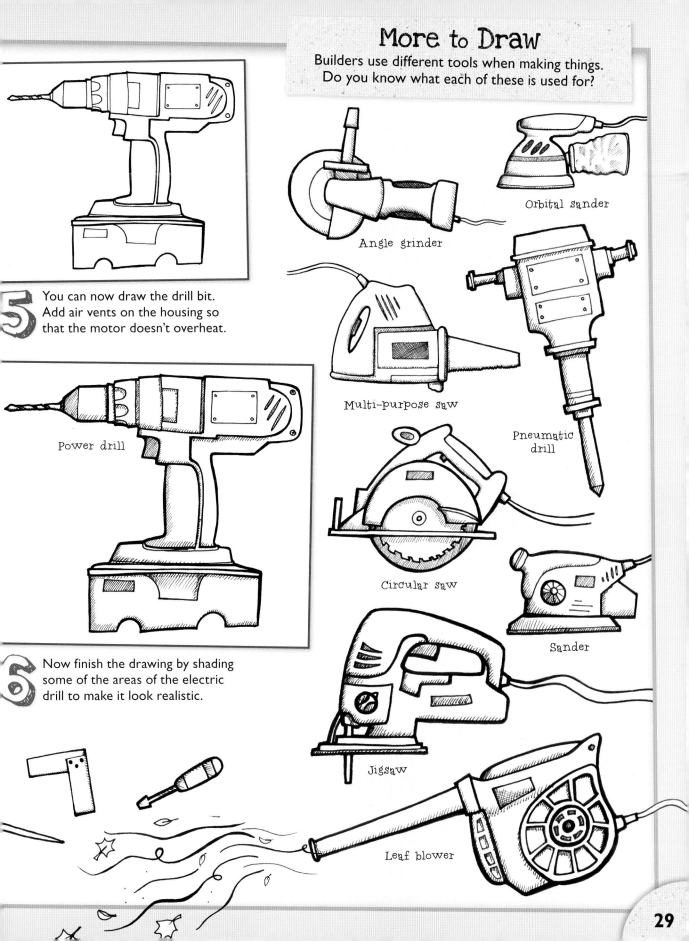

More to Draw

Builders use different tools when making things.
Do you know what each of these is used for?

5 You can now draw the drill bit.
Add air vents on the housing so
that the motor doesn't overheat.

Power drill

6 Now finish the drawing by shading
some of the areas of the electric
drill to make it look realistic.

Angle grinder

Orbital sander

Multi-purpose saw

Pneumatic drill

Circular saw

Sander

Jigsaw

Leaf blower

Music Equipment

Playing music on turntables is a cool thing to do. Skilled DJs can blend two records together so you don't notice when one finishes and the next starts.

1 Start by drawing two circles for the turntables inside a large oval shape.

2 Draw small circles inside and larger circles around the turntables. Now create a panel at the front.

3 Draw lines from the turntables t the panel and a monitor stand.

Television

Hi-fi system

Digital radio

Gramophone

Now add some buttons, switches and a big monitor.

Mixing decks

Finish the drawing by shading some areas to highlight them. Add a reflection to the screen.

Headphones

Draw more buttons and knobs. Also add two small speakers attached to the turntables by wires.

Speaker stand

Portable Stereo

Index

There are loads of exciting things to draw in this book. Practice your new-found drawing skills by adding some of them to your drawings.